Sugaring Season

Making Maple Syrup

Sugaring Season

Making Maple Syrup

by Diane L. Burns
photographs by
Cheryl Walsh Bellville

Carolrhoda Books, Inc./Minneapolis

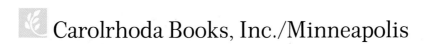

The author extends thanks to the following people for their help in making this book possible: Bea and Dury Miller; The Proctor Research Center at the University of Vermont (especially Sumner Williams and Harry Yawney); Christy Hauge, Forestry Specialist at the University of Wisconsin at Stevens Point; Bill Moore; Scott Wood; Debbie Richards; and Phil Burns. In addition, a hearty thank-you goes to the many U.S. sugar bush owners/producers who responded to my questionnaire.

Special thanks to Anderson's Sugar Bush for allowing its employees, products, and packaging processes to be photographed, pages 2, 10-11, 38-41.

LIBRARY OF CONGRESS CATALOGING-IN-PUBLICATION DATA

Burns, Diane L.
    Sugaring Season: making maple syrup / Diane Burns; photographs by Cheryl Walsh Bellville
        p.   cm.
    Summary: Describes, in text and photographs, the making of maple syrup from tapping the tree and collecting the sap to cooking and packaging.
    1. Maple syrup—Juvenile literature. [1. Maple syrup.]
I. Bellville, Cheryl Walsh, photo. II. Title.
TP395.B87 1990
664'.132—dc20   89-48513
                                                              CIP
                                                              AC

ISBN 0-87614-422-9

Manufactured in the United States of America

1 2 3 4 5 6 7 8 9 10   99 98 97 96 95 94 93 92 91 90

*For all those who wait patiently
for the maple moon and carry
on the sugaring tradition,
most especially for Phil,
who sweetens my life* —D.L.B.

For Nonny, with love —C.W.B.

Contents

The Trees   5
The Sap   8
The Sugar Bush   10
The Preparations   15
The Tapping   18
The Run   22
The Cooking   25
The Grading   33
The Packaging   38
The Season's End   42
Author's Note   47
Glossary   48

The Trees

In the frosty January dawn, the maple trees in Dury Miller's woods stand like soldiers at attention. Snow sits stubbornly in drifts at their feet. Icy crystals remain frozen in the thin warmth of the late-winter sun. Yet the days stretch slowly toward springtime.

5

Soon rising temperatures will trigger the beginning of sugaring season. Maple syrup makers in northern and central United States, from Maine to Minnesota, and in southeastern Canada will begin collecting sap from sugar maple trees. This sap will then be boiled down into syrup.

Maple syrup is made only in North America, though some maples are found in Europe and Asia. There are several different kinds of maple trees, but most maple syrup is made from the sap of the sugar maple, or hard maple. The scientific name for this maple is *Acer saccharum.*

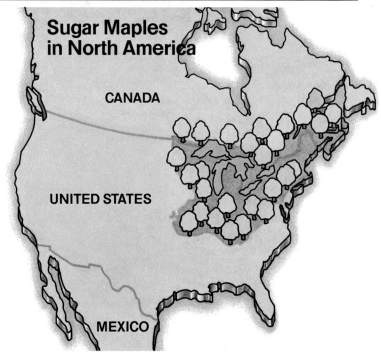

Sugar Maples in North America

CANADA

UNITED STATES

MEXICO

Sugar maples are easy to find in the woods. Their leaves have a distinctive three-part shape. Each part has three points. In autumn, these leaves make a dazzling display in bright shades of yellow or red gold.

The Sap

Sap is a tree's lifeblood. It is a watery liquid that contains sugars and minerals. These sugars are the tree's food. During winter, while the tree is at rest, the sap is stored in the roots.

As winter grows old, days grow warmer. Temperatures rise above freezing in the daytime and drop below freezing at night. During this short time of year, a tree's sap flows up and down with the temperature. While the sun is out, the sap flows upward to the stems and branches where it is warm. The sap is food for the developing leaf buds. As the sun goes down and the temperature falls, so does the sap, flowing back into the roots.

During the day, the sap flows up toward the stems and branches.

In the evening, the sap flows down to the roots.

Sugaring season begins when this up-and-down movement of sap happens for several days in a row. This stretch of days is called a **run.** The run generally lasts from 10 days to 6 weeks, with sap flowing more on some days than on others.

Runs usually occur during March and April, and again in September and October. The sap in the fall, though, is not as sweet as in the spring.

The Sugar Bush

Dury Miller owns a 59-acre grove of maple trees. A woods like this, consisting mostly of maple trees, is called a **sugar bush**. Dury does not farm the sugar bush, so he rents it to Phil Burns. In return, Phil gives him a portion of the season's syrup.

This sugar bush can hold about 7,000 **tapholes**. A taphole is a hole, about the size of a man's thumb, drilled into a tree's trunk to remove sap. Large trees can have more than one taphole. So a sugar bush's size is measured by the number of tapholes it can support—not the number of trees growing there.

Syrup makers long ago—the Native Americans and pioneers—first tapped maples by making gashes in the trees. This **gashing**, though, was dangerous to the trees. It left them open to insects and diseases. Few people gather sap this way now.

In the 19th century, people began drilling holes into the trees. Then they would place a grooved piece of branch in the hole for a spout. A wooden bucket was hung under each spout to collect the sap. Afterward, the syrup makers hauled the sap, bucket by bucket, to a tank on a wagon or to the place where the sap would be cooked. This method took a great deal of energy and many workers.

Some syrup makers still rely on this centuries-old bucket method. But now they use metal **tap-spouts** and plastic buckets.

Many modern syrup farms, like Dury Miller's, use a **vacuum-tubing system**. The system collects sap with a network of plastic tubing, a set of vacuum pumps, and stainless-steel storage tanks. Using this method, farmers can harvest more sap than with the bucket-drip method. The suction from the **vacuum pumps** gently draws the sap from the trees, even on cloudy days when the sap doesn't drip on its own. Sap collected through plastic tubing is also cleaner than sap collected by buckets. The tubing helps to protect the sap from insects, molds, and dirt.

Phil

Wayne

Dury

Jim

Phil needs eight miles of plastic tubing to connect his 7,000 tapholes. To manage all these tapholes and lines, Phil uses a crew of two to four people. Jim and Wayne are this year's crew. Dury will come over to help if another person is needed.

The Preparations

During February, Phil and his crew prepare for the sap harvest. They use chain saws to cut down unhealthy or storm-damaged trees. Removing these trees gives healthy trees more room for growth. Sugar maples that have plenty of room yield, or give out, more and sweeter sap than crowded maples.

The crew also inspects the **syrup house** (sometimes called the evaporating shed or sugarhouse). The sap will be cooked into syrup in this building.

Afterward, the men walk slowly through the bush, examining the **main lines**. These pipes of sturdy plastic run throughout the sugar bush. Once the season begins, the main lines will carry large quantities of sap from the different areas of the sugar bush to the holding tanks. These pipes remain in place all year, and they must be checked each season for sags and holes.

As the crew members walk and work, squirrels and other chewing rodents are on their minds. Last summer, these gnawing animals ruined all the tubing in the sugar bush. A season's profits were spent on repair and new tubing.

After last year's disaster, the crew carefully applied a paste made of spicy peppers to all the new and old tubing to keep the squirrels away. And it worked! The syrup farm will not lose profits to the pesky squirrels this year.

The Tapping

February moves crisply into March, and the weather softens. Sugaring season cannot be far away, so Wayne and Jim begin to tap the trees. They carry a portable drill and a hammer with them. The two men work as a team, moving from tree to tree.

To tap a tree without harming it, the tree must be at least 50 years old. It must have a trunk 31½ inches around (10 inches in diameter) when measured 4½ feet above the ground. A trunk this wide can safely handle one taphole. A 44-inch trunk (14 inches in diameter) can support two tapholes, and a 56½-inch trunk (18 inches in diameter) can take three. Syrup makers add one taphole to a tree for every 12½ additional inches around the trunk (4 inches in diameter). Over the years, people who tap trees learn to judge the size of a tree's trunk just by looking at it.

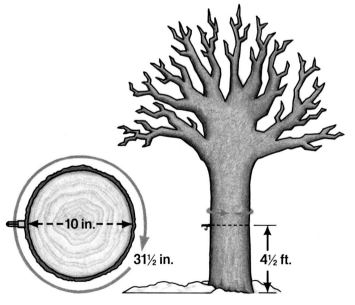

Tapping removes only a small portion of a tree's sap. Tapholes placed according to these guidelines do not shorten the life of a tree. After the sugaring season, the sugar maples heal themselves by closing each hole with additional bark and scar tissue.

Each taphole yields about 10 gallons of sap over the course of a season. This amount of sap cooks down to about one quart of maple syrup. Phil and his crew hope to cook about 70,000 gallons of sap into more than 1,700 gallons of maple syrup.

The **flow**, or amount of running sap, is not greatly affected by which side of the tree is tapped or by how high the tap is from the ground. So Wayne estimates the depth of the snow beneath him and chooses a comfortable height for himself. He knows that tapholes drilled eight feet above the ground are easy to reach from a snowdrift in March—but they are impossible to remove in April when the drift has melted!

Wayne drills each taphole 2 inches deep with a $7/16$-inch drill bit. He spaces the proper number of tapholes carefully around the tree and avoids putting a new taphole too near the scars of an old one.

Jim follows Wayne, plugging tap-spouts into the holes by gently knocking them into position with a hammer. He is careful not to split the trunk's bark. The tree will heal more easily because of this care.

Every tap-spout is attached to a slender piece of plastic tubing, which looks like a miniature garden hose. This tap line is then connected to a common hose for each tree. The tree lines eventually connect into the main lines, which are larger.

In four days, Phil's experienced crew has drilled and connected all 7,000 tapholes. Slender green hoses now join the trees in the sugar bush together in a huge connect-the-dots pattern.

The Run

A week passes, then another. Phil continues to wait for the special weather conditions needed for sugaring season.

Finally, in late March, it comes. The weather forecasters predict a long spell of warm, sunny days with cool, freezing nights.

The next morning, Phil and his crew waken to the drip, drip, drip of melting snow, and they hurry out to check the lines. The first sap of the season is dripping from the tap-spouts into the tubing.

Sugaring season has begun!

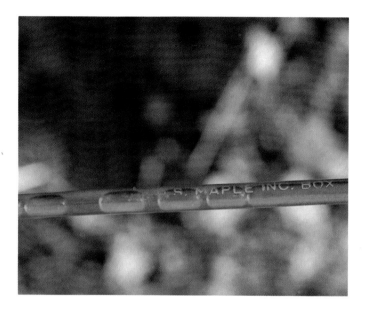

Phil switches on the vacuum pumps. Gentle suction coaxes clear sap from each tree. Phil will run the pumps as long as the sap flows. Night usually brings an end to the day's sap flow, and the pumps are shut off.

On this first morning, Phil walks along the tubing lines. He listens for a suck-and-whoosh sound and watches for swiftly moving air bubbles inside the tubing. Both are signs of air leaks that must be repaired for the vacuum system to work well.

At some sugar bushes, no suction is needed because the syrup house is built in a low spot. All the tubing lines slope to the syrup house, and the sap simply flows downhill to be collected.

At hilly sugar bushes, like Dury's, the syrup house sits in the middle of the grove. Special stainless-steel storage tanks are set between the hills in each of the bush's low spots. Each tank holds as much as 500 gallons of fresh sap.

Once the holding tanks begin to fill, the fresh sap is pumped to the main storage tank behind the syrup house. This must be done quickly so the sap won't spoil.

Some syrup makers move the sap with tractors, horses, or trucks. Phil uses electric pumps to move the sap uphill through plastic pipes to the syrup house. There the sap is stored in a 10,000-gallon tank.

Although sap is mostly water, the amount and mixture of sugars and minerals in the sap varies from tree to tree and year to year. Sugar maples that have had a good summer—with plenty of water, good soil, sunshine, and room to grow—have a sweeter sap than those that have had a poor growing season. Sweeter sap requires less boiling to make it into syrup.

Phil tests the raw sap in the storage tank with a **sap hydrometer**, an instrument that measures the amount of sugar in the sap. Most sugar maples yield a sap with two to eight percent sugar content. This batch measures four percent.

The Cooking

When sap has been spurting through the lines all day, there is no time to relax.

Phil's main storage tank fills ever higher— 1,000 gallons, 2,000, 6,000. Jim and Wayne leave for an evening of well-deserved rest, while Phil remains behind to cook the sap collected that day.

The cooking is done in **evaporating pans**—a series of shallow rectangular pans set over open flames. As the sap cooks, water in the sap evaporates. This is the reason it takes so much sap to make syrup—because great amounts of water are lost in evaporation. A thick liquid with concentrated amounts of cooked sugars and minerals is left behind. This sweet liquid is maple syrup!

To cut down on cooking time, some large sugar bushes (15,000 or more tapholes) are equipped with a high-technology filtering system that separates the sugars and minerals in the sap from the water. After the filtering, the sugars and minerals are boiled to change them into syrup.

Phil pumps the cold, clear sap from the main tank into the syrup house. The sap winds through a series of copper coils above the evaporator pans. Once the cooking has begun, the rising steam will preheat the sap in the coils. The warmed sap will then boil more quickly when it reaches the pans.

Phil's syrup house has a set of two evaporating pans. Each pan is divided into small

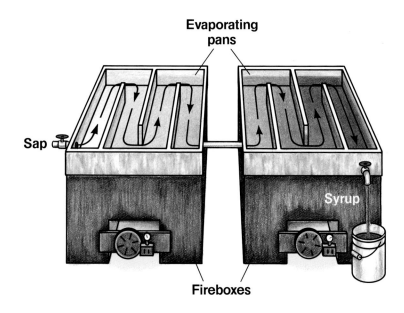

channels like a maze, and the two pans are connected with a hose and a pump. The water in the sap evaporates quickly in these pans because small amounts of sap are spread over a large heating area.

Many syrup makers have sets of three or more evaporating pans. The number and size of the pans doesn't change the taste of the syrup. It just affects how quickly the syrup cooks.

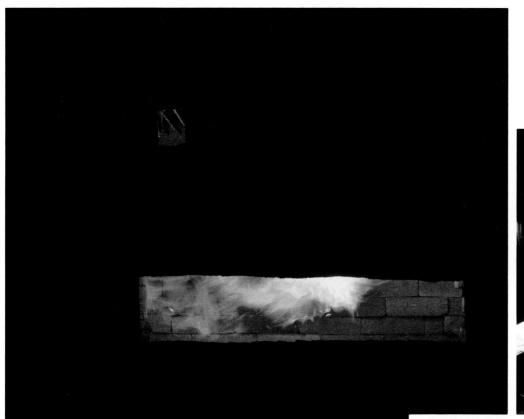

Underneath each evaporating pan is a **firebox** that houses the flames that heat the pans. Many syrup makers use wood fires. Others, like Phil, use oil or natural gas burners. With modern equipment, Phil has more control over the cooking temperature, and he doesn't need to spend time cutting or hauling wood.

28

Phil turns the storage-tank valve, and sap flows into the first evaporating pan and winds into the second. Once the syrup reaches the two-inch level in both pans, Phil turns off the valve and turns on the heat. With this much sap in the pans, the sap won't scorch as it boils. A floating switch keeps the sap at this safe level by letting more sap into the first pan as the sap cooks down.

After a few hours, Phil will begin drawing off finished syrup. As sap is added to the first pan and syrup is removed from the second, a slow current starts to flow through the two-pan system. The sap will wind its way through the maze of the two pans, growing heavier and hotter as it cooks, until it is finished syrup.

The sap boils quickly with the intense heat from the roaring fire. Bubbles foam up, bringing **impurities**, such as dirt and tiny pieces of bark, to the surface. Phil skims off the foam and keeps a close eye on the sap level.

As the sap cooks, great clouds of steam billow up, ballooning out through the syrup house's roof. A thick maple-sweet smell rises with the steam.

Phil keeps the firebox burning steadily and as hot as possible. He watches for the syrup to be finished, and he catnaps when he can.

About three hours later, in the early hours of morning, the first sap has thickened until it is nearly finished. Maple syrup is usually ready when it reaches 7°F above the boiling point of water. This is often 219°F, but if the air pressure rises or drops, the boiling point of water changes. So syrup makers have to keep an eye on their **barometers**, which measure atmospheric pressure.

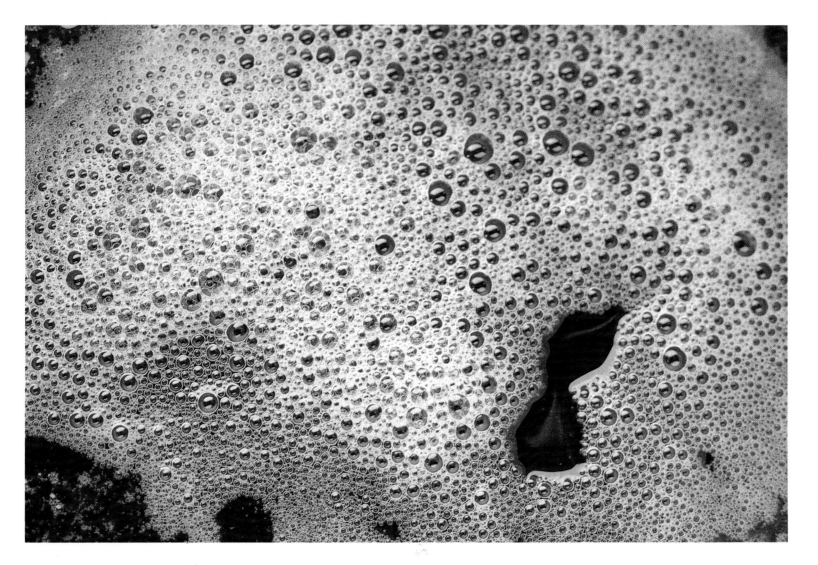

Syrup makers can see when the syrup is ready, or nearly so, by pulling out a dipper of the liquid and letting it pour off the ladle's edge. If the syrup runs together in a thick sheet, it is said to be sheeting, curtaining, or aproning. This sheeting action is a sign that the syrup may be done.

To make sure, Phil pours a sample of syrup into a bucket. He fills a long narrow cup. Inside it, he places a special glass tube, called a **syrup hydrometer**. If the hydrometer floats at a certain level, the sugar in the syrup is the correct **density**, or concentration. If it sinks or does not float high enough, the syrup's sugar is not concentrated, or heavy, enough.

Properly finished syrup weighs just over 11 pounds per gallon. If the syrup is cooked beyond this point, it may crystallize or scorch. If the syrup is not cooked long enough, it may be too thin and spoil quickly.

After using the syrup hydrometer, Phil pulls out a **Brix syrup refractometer** to double-check his findings. This instrument measures the percent of sugar in the hot syrup. It must be 66% or above to be finished. Phil puts one drop of syrup in the end and holds it up to the light. The first batch measures 66%. It's done!

The Grading

Phil opens the spout on the second evaporating pan, and steaming syrup pours out. He then strains the syrup by pouring it, bucket by bucket, through a **filter**. The filter is usually made of a layer or several layers of a material with small holes. Some sugar makers use wool, felt, cheesecloth, or paper filters. Others use a filter press. The metal plates in a filter press squeeze the syrup through many layers of waffled paper or cloth.

Filtering removes a sugary sand, called **niter**. Niter is made up of minerals that have settled into small grains during the cooking process. The darker the syrup, the more niter the syrup has.

After the syrup is filtered, it is poured into stainless-steel holding tanks. Once again, Phil moves the steaming syrup, bucket by bucket. By sunup, his arms ache.

The next step in the process is **grading**, or classifying a batch of syrup according to government standards for color, flavor, and density. Grading is important because it determines the price of the syrup.

Phil pours some of the new syrup into a clear bottle and matches this sample against the bottles in his grading kit. The standard colors are light, medium, and dark amber. Syrups that match these colors are all Grade A table syrups. These syrups can be sold anywhere. But the lighter-colored Grade A syrups are better because their flavors are usually more delicate. A higher price per pound can be charged for light- and medium-amber syrups.

Syrups that are darker than amber can have a stronger, often bitter maple flavor. These darker syrups are generally sold to commercial bakeries or food-processing plants. They may also be combined with lighter-colored syrups for a desired shade of amber. Many food-processing plants add darker syrups to corn syrup and sell the combination as an inexpensive pancake syrup.

Syrup makers cannot control the color of the syrup. It is highly dependent on the mixture of sugars and minerals in the sap, as well as the time of the season. Many times the first syrup of the season is lighter than the last.

Later in the morning, Jim and Wayne return to take over for their weary boss. The Millers also drop in to see how the syrup is cooking.

They're all just in time. More syrup has reached the finished stage. One batch is a lighter amber than the other. Now is the time for the real test—the taste test.

The Miller's granddaughter, Monique, is the official taste tester. She takes a sip of each sample and smiles. They're both mighty tasty!

The next morning, a pitcher of the season's first syrup is the guest of honor at the breakfast table. The Millers, their guests, and all the crew sit down for the traditional sausage-and-pancake breakfast before another day of syrup making begins.

The Pckaging

The work continues, and the crew is busier than ever. After the first batch of syrup is done, more syrup is ready every half hour. The crew must now handle two jobs—cooking the sap and packaging the syrup.

Maple syrup must be packaged while it is hot. Otherwise it must be reheated, skimmed, and filtered again. Sometimes, if the crew doesn't have time to package all the syrup immediately, the extra syrup is stored under a special light that keeps it from spoiling. This kind of cool storage, however, darkens the syrup over a long period of time, so Phil uses it only for short periods.

Like other sugar farmers, Phil packages his maple syrup for several different purposes. He fills quart and pint bottles and containers for gift shops and grocery stores. These bottles are labeled and then packed in sturdy cartons for shipping.

Phil also sends 55-gallon drums and 5-gallon pails of maple syrup by semi-trailer trucks to restaurants, bakeries, and stores.

Not all farmers package and sell their own syrup. About ¾ of the maple syrup made each year is sold by farmers to companies that package and sell the syrup. These packaging companies are able to ship the syrup to customers around the world. Each year, more and more maple syrup finds its way to breakfast tables in Japan, Germany, and many other countries.

Many sugar bushes use specially designed packages and labels for their products. Although Phil sells only syrup, other farmers use a part of their syrup to make and sell additional maple products, such as maple sugar, maple candy, and maple cream (maple syrup whipped until it's light, like creamy honey). There is even maple-coated popcorn and maple cotton candy!

Some syrup makers make a traditional sweet called maple sugar-on-snow for themselves and their children. They boil the new syrup until it reaches a high temperature (about 275°F). Then they pour the hot syrup onto a clean patch of snow. The syrup cools quickly into a chewy, taffylike candy.

The Season's End

Sugaring season draws to a close when the weather stays above freezing both day and night. Sap stops flowing after 36 straight hours of above-freezing weather. Only a new frost can bring it back.

As the run draws to a close, the syrup maker must watch the maple trees carefully. The flow of sap may still be high, but after the buds on the branches swell and burst, the sap changes. The clear liquid becomes cloudy and less sweet.

The syrup made from this late-season sap is of lower quality and is called **buddy**. It has a stronger, more bitter flavor. Because of this, farmers judge the end of the season by the budding of the maple trees—not by the end of the run.

When Phil suspects that the time of budding is near, he takes a long walk in the woods. He listens for birds. Have the crows returned? He checks other woody plants. Are they ready to bud? The sugar maker finds clues to how long the sap will be of high quality by watching the activities of animals and other plants. Some maple syrup makers also keep an eye on the moon. A full moon may bring another frost and a longer sugaring season.

After just nine days, this year's season comes to an end. Phil's crew pulls all the taps from the trees in one day. Then they start the long job of disconnecting, draining, and cleaning the lines and the cooking equipment to prepare them for storage. It's a busy time.

As the men work, they take inventory. Finally, when all is ready to be put away, the crew spreads the spicy-pepper paste on the tubing and tap sets. This should keep unwanted visitors away for another year.

The work is done. Reluctantly, Phil shutters the syrup house windows and padlocks the door. A whole year will come and go before the harvest of maple sap begins again. Like other syrup makers, he'll miss working outdoors and the quiet companionship of trees and coworkers. As the other farmers do, he'll look forward to next year's challenge of making this age-old treat with a curious mix of tradition and technology.

Phil thinks back. This was a short season and late in coming. But it was sweet, very sweet. A total of 1,800 gallons of quality syrup were made. Soon people all around the world will be sitting down to a delightful breakfast of pancakes and pure maple syrup. It is a job well done.

Author's Note

The sugar bush is closed for the season, but Phil does not stop thinking about the woods. Like wise syrup makers everywhere, Phil cares for his trees year-round. Without healthy trees, there is no harvest.

In recent years, farmers in both Canada and the United States have reported that some of their trees are dying. They do not fully understand why. Scientists have begun studying the problem. They suspect that the deaths of the maples are due to the stresses of pollution, such as acid rain, combined with the stress of difficult weather conditions, such as drought.

Sugar bushes face other threats as well. Insects often harm sugar maples. Pear thrips are insects so small that they are hard to see until they have caused damage to the trees. They eat the trees' leaf buds in the spring. Without healthy leaves, the weakened maples grow poorly and yield less sap. Rodents, and sometimes vandals, also damage maples in various ways.

Research into these problems, and others, is being carried out at several experiment centers in Canada and the United States. Scientists are at work to develop new types of maple trees that grow faster, are more resistant to insects and disease, and yield a sweeter sap. In addition, they search for better ways to harvest and cook the maple sap, so syrup makers like Phil can make the best use of their time.

The North American tradition of making maple syrup has lasted for over 300 years. The legacy continues today because of the work of many different people: the sugar makers who care for their trees, the scientists who study ways to keep the maple groves thriving, and the citizens who make choices for a clean and healthy environment.

Glossary

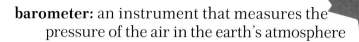

barometer: an instrument that measures the pressure of the air in the earth's atmosphere

Brix syrup refractometer: an instrument that measures the percent of sugar in hot maple syrup

buddy: a term describing syrup made from the sap of trees that have already budded

density: the concentration or percent of sugar in the syrup

evaporating pans: a series of shallow, rectangular pans that are divided into narrow channels and used for the continuous cooking of sap

filter: a material—such as wool, felt, or cheese-cloth—that is used to strain the hot syrup

firebox: a container under the evaporating pans used to enclose the open flames

flow: the amount of sap that drips from a tap-hole during a run

gashing: an unhealthy, old-time method of tree tapping. After a few years of such treatment, the trees often die.

grade: to classify a batch of syrup by comparing its color to the color standards provided by the government (United States or Canada). The sample's color, along with its density and flavor, determines its quality and price.

impurities: things not naturally a part of syrup

main lines: sturdy plastic pipes that carry large volumes of raw sap to the storage tanks and syrup house

niter: sugar sand—a gritty deposit of sugar and minerals found in unfiltered maple syrup

run: consecutive days in spring and fall when the maple tree's sap travels upward to the branches during the warm days and descends into the roots during the freezing nights

sap hydrometer: an instrument used to measure the percent of sugar in raw sap

sugar bush: a grove of maple trees, usually being farmed for maple sap

syrup house: the building at the sugar bush where the sap is cooked down into syrup

syrup hydrometer: an instrument used to measure the weight of sugar solids in hot syrup

tapholes: holes that are drilled into the trunk of maple trees to remove sap

tap-spouts: spouts placed into tapholes to channel the flow of sap

vacuum pumps: machines that remove air from tubing lines and create suction

vacuum-tubing system: the method of collecting sap with a network of plastic tubes and vacuum suction